When it was announced that Baudouin, the 'Bachelor King', had finally chosen his future Queen, the Belgian public responded with relief, rather than dismay at Fabiola's Spanish origin. The couple's deep and lasting love was to act as a buffer against the private and political misfortunes that troubled their marriage – and their anguish at being denied a child.

FATAL ACCIDENTS

BAUDOUIN'S EARLY CHILDHOOD WAS OVERSHADOWED BY TWO TRAGIC DEATHS – BOTH RELATED TO THE FAMILY'S PASSION FOR CLIMBING – AND THIS MADE THE SERIOUS YOUNG PRINCE SEEM MATURE BEYOND HIS AGE

Hulton Picture Company

THE AFTERNOON OF 7 SEPTEMBER 1930 FOUND Prince Leopold of Belgium nervously pacing the grounds of Stuyvenberg Palace alongside his father, King Albert. It had been a tiring summer: on 21 July, Belgium had celebrated the centennial anniversary of its independence. Since then the kingdom had enjoyed a seemingly endless succession of festivities. And for Leopold, 7 September seemed more tiring than any of the arduous days that had preceded it.

That morning, the 29-year-old Prince had set out in one of his many fast cars to inaugurate a monument at Dixmund. But just before he reached his destination he had received a telegram commanding him to take the first train back to Brussels. Now, he was waiting on tenterhooks for news to come from the Palace, where his wife Astrid was in labour. At 4.25 pm his vigil ceased, when it was announced that Astrid had given birth to a boy. As the sound of church bells and artillery cannonades rang out around the capital, the people of Belgium once more flung themselves into celebration. The ruling house of Coburg had a male heir.

Truly Belgian

Just one hour after his birth, the young Prince was privately baptized as Baudouin Leopold Albert Charles Axel Marie Gustave. King Albert, who stood as godfather, was pleased with his son's choice. 'A truly *Belgian* name,' he remarked of Baudouin. And, the following day, the newborn Prince's grandmother, Princess Ingeborg of Sweden, formally presented the

⚜ *The enormous popularity Prince Leopold and Princess Astrid below enjoyed with the Belgian people was reflected in the nation's jubilant celebrations at the births of their children Josephine-Charlotte and Baudouin left. Despite the tragedies in his early years, at play Baudouin right was much like any other child. He adored all things mechanical and his bedroom was plastered with pictures of trains and planes*

child to the Burgomaster of Brussels.

It was a popular birth, and not only for the national holiday that accompanied it. Prince Leopold, Duke of Brabant and heir presumptive to the Belgian throne, was all that a prince should be as far as the public were concerned. Born in 1901, he had enjoyed a happy childhood. In an age when children were to be seen and not heard, the devotion of his parents, Albert and Elisabeth, to their children was a welcome change. 'In Germany, men have other matters to engage their attention,' barked one visiting

Popperfoto

JERUSALEM

The name Baudouin holds a prestigious position in Belgium's past. In the 11th and 12th centuries, when crusaders poured east to fight the 'infidel', those from Flanders accounted well for themselves. It was a Baudouin who, in 1098, had created the first Crusader State at Edessa. The same Baudouin later went on to become the first King of Jerusalem. And it was one of his descendants who staved off the attacks of the great Muslim warrior Saladin.

The fighting men of Flanders left a sturdy legacy of their ambition − the Kingdom of Jerusalem was to last for almost 200 years. And they enjoyed the fruits of their conquests to the full. While Europe's nobility huddled in their woollen cloaks and dark castles, the inhabitants of Outremer, as the Crusader States were called, lived a life of free and easy luxury

---

Prussian prince. 'I have noticed it,' replied Albert, 'without envy.' During World War 1 Leopold endeared himself to his people by enlisting in the army as a simple private, and as he grew older he matured into a figure that seemed to have sprung from a fairy-tale. Fair-haired, broad-shouldered and good-looking, he was an active sportsman who loved swimming, skiing, climbing, golf and fast cars. But while the scions of other dynasties were gaining reputations as royal *roués*, the Belgians were pleased to note that their Prince had a strong sense of royal duty.

The Snow Princess

Their admiration for him was further enhanced in 1926, when he brought home from Stockholm his 20-year-old bride, Princess Astrid of Sweden. 'The Snow Princess', as an adoring public immediately nicknamed her, was a perfect partner for the Golden Prince. She was beautiful, graceful, relaxed and yet remarkably formal. 'Whenever that exquisite lady talked to you she made you feel assured, interesting and terrifically liked!' recalled one admirer who had enjoyed the warmth of Astrid's unequalled charm.

Nor was Astrid's charm reserved only for royalty or aristocracy. When her first child, Josephine-Charlotte, was born in 1927, she would wheel the pram through the public park, stopping to talk with other mothers. When Baudouin arrived three years later, it was no different. It was clear to the Belgians that their Royal Family was very much one of them.

It was in this golden haze of popularity that the young Prince Baudouin spent his early childhood. Every year he would accompany his mother on a long holiday spent amidst the lakes and forests of Sweden. And sometimes the

'Never were children loved more than were the children of Queen Astrid'

A JOURNALIST ON BAUDOUIN'S CHILDHOOD

🜲 *King Albert was famous for his rock-climbing* right *and it was fitting that he should meet his end while pursuing his favourite sport. On a cold day in February 1934, Albert decided to take a bracing climb but failed to rejoin his valet at the appointed time. A search-party eventually found the King after midnight, his head crushed by a fall, and his belongings scattered around him. The tragedy of his death was felt as much by the Belgian people as by his grandson Baudouin*

whole family would go to their lakeside estate at Kussnacht, near Lucerne. At the age of three he made his first official appearance at the launching of a new vessel from the Hoboken ship yards. Observers saw a diminutive, white-haired figure dressed in a white sailor's costume, who appeared to be at the same time serious and smiling, with an occasional flash of mischief.

The smiles were soon to disappear. In February 1934, King Albert died in a climbing accident. And on the 23rd Baudouin stood by his father's side to see him crowned Leopold III. Even at that age, it was noticed, the young, blond Prince seemed unusually quiet and serious. Baudouin was rapidly coming to terms with life.

Family life

But for the moment all seemed well in the House of Coburg. On 6 June 1934, Astrid gave birth to another son, Albert. And the nation revelled in photographs such as that of Baudouin, peering on tip-toe into his younger brother's lace-bedecked cot. It seemed a perfect, happy family. Their life was simple: at Stuyvenberg they dined as a group, with Astrid serving from a side trolley. Besides excursions to Brussels' public parks she took them on shopping expeditions to the capital's department stores. And when not accompanying her husband abroad, she would take the children to Sweden or Kussnacht.

But in the summer of 1935, tragedy struck. Having spent an agreeable week climbing in the Dolomites, Leopold and Astrid went to spend a few days at Kussnacht. The morning of Thursday 29 August was warm and pleasant, the perfect day, so the Royal couple thought, for climbing. By ten o'clock they were in the car and heading for the mountains. Leopold – who

👑Above *Very much a natural mother, Queen Astrid tried to spend as much time with her children as she could possibly spare. Her untimely death seemed to deprive them of part of their childhood*

👑Left *The scene of the accident. By the time Leopold's car plunged into the lake after skidding down the embankment, both he and his wife had been thrown out*

👑Below *The people of Belgium pay their last respects to the young Queen who was so universally adored. King Leopold is said to have walked the full four miles of the funeral procession*

EMPRESS CARLOTA

The Belgian Queens seemed to be dogged by unhappiness. But perhaps the most tragic of all Coburg women was Empress Carlota. In 1857, Princess Charlotte of Belgium had married the Austrian Archduke Maximilian. It was a happy marriage, one of the few in the 19th century forged by love rather than politics. But in 1863, French arms and money thrust them onto the Mexican throne. It spelt disaster for both their marriage and the new dynasty.

Empress Carlota, as she now was, remained childless, and Maximilian began to take a string of mistresses. After his execution in 1867, Carlota went insane and was to spend the next 60 years incarcerated in the Château de Tervueren. She died in solitary misery in 1927

Popperfoto

for once was driving at a sedate pace – turned to ask Astrid for directions, and at that point he lost control. The car mounted the curb, then skidded down the embankment. Battered and bruised, and with his right arm broken, Leopold staggered to where Astrid lay. Although she had a fractured skull she was still alive. But by the time the doctors arrived there was nothing they could do. The local priest came just in time to administer the last sacraments before Astrid died in her husband's arms.

A nation in mourning

Five days later, Astrid's hearse was drawn through the streets of Brussels by eight black-plumed horses. As church bells tolled, the Belgian people packed the pavements to watch in silence the passing of their Queen. Behind the hearse, as it made its way from the Church of St Gudule to the family vaults at Laeken, walked the solitary figure of Leopold. For the full four-mile distance he paced along, his arm in a black sling. Onlookers saw their King sway in pain as he

King Leopold tried to keep his children out of the limelight for many months following their mother's death. But on Independence Day 1938 the Royal Family re-appeared in public below to watch Belgian troops and servicemen march past

Hulton Picture Company

Parc. It was under his supervision that Baudouin received his education, spending hours of study alongside four other children, carefully picked from different classes of society, in a special schoolroom in the Royal Palace.

Despite the tragedies that had devastated his earlier years, it seemed that Baudouin was following a fairly normal route to maturity. But then, in September 1939, war broke out, and on 10 May 1940 the German blitzkrieg swept into the Low Countries. As Germany presented her declaration of war to Foreign Minister Paul Spaak, bombs were already falling on Belgium.

War takes over

Leopold immediately took over personal command of the armed forces. The children, however, accompanied only by Gatien du Parc, two tutors and a handful of servants, joined the millions of refugees streaming south into France. On 22 May, they alighted at Lot in southern France, where they stayed in the Château de Montalm. It was a gloomy place whose dreary aura reached over the whole group. Baudouin fell ill, and while he was still recuperating he learned that Belgium had capitulated on 28 May. It was a moment of deep depression. Leopold knew nothing of what had happened to his children, and they in turn knew nothing of their father's fate.

In despair, Gatien du Parc decided to take his charges to a place of greater safety. And for six weeks the Royal refugees billeted themselves at San Sebastian, on the northern shores of Spain. As the children anxiously listened for news from the front – which by June was at the English Channel – they picked away despondently at an impromptu series of Spanish lessons.

walked, occasionally wiping a tear from his eye. It was obvious to all that he had suffered a shattering blow.

But he was not alone in his suffering. 'Never,' wrote one journalist, 'were children loved more than were the children of Queen Astrid, in those days when the whole of Belgium was bowed under its unspeakable loss.' The 14-month-old Albert could barely have known his mother. But for Baudouin and his elder sister Josephine-Charlotte it was the end of an era, the end of those peaceful days within the white walls of Stuyvenberg. To Leopold it was a place 'that had lost all its warmth and light'. The Palace was closed, its locked doors guarding Astrid's memory, and the King and his children moved into the nearby Palace at Laeken.

A new home

For a long time Baudouin and the others kept out of the public eye. But even when they re-emerged from mourning it took a long time for the grief to wear off. Baudouin had always been serious, but now the smiles that had alleviated his gravity were not to be seen.

There were, however, plenty of things to distract him from his sorrow, such as his indefatigable grandmother, Queen Elisabeth, who plied him with heartening anecdotes about King Albert. And in 1936 he was put under the supervision of a governor, the Viscount Gatien du

♛ *Happy days for Albert with Swedish 'granny' Princess Ingeborg* above. *Two devoted grandmothers tried to make up for the loss of Queen Astrid*

♛ **Below** *A nine-year-old Prince Baudouin reviews future naval officers at Ostend*

Lynne Robinson

Fifteen-foot long veil of ivory tulle secured by a Spanish coronet

♛ *Left* Fabiola was a winter bride, married on 15 December 1960. Her dress has clearly been influenced by the great Spanish designer Balenciaga, with its uncluttered outline and almost complete absence of detail. The total effect, softened by the long, full veil and lavish use of ermine, is quite stunning

Boat-shaped neckline trimmed with ermine - the fur of royalty

Gown of ivory satin flares out from the waist into a softly gathered full skirt

♛ *Right* Fabiola attends an afternoon reception at the Belgian Embassy in London, in 1963. She is wearing what is almost the Royal 'uniform' for daytime engagements: a hat set well off the face and long white gloves. Her elaborate dress, which is made of pale lime silk chiffon scattered with sequins, would probably be more appropriate as an evening-dress, were it not being worn by a Queen

♛ This beautiful satin evening-dress *top right* sets off Fabiola's dark Spanish looks to perfection. The Empire line, first seen at the court of the Empress Josephine in the early 19th century, was revived in the late 'sixties and became very popular

♛ The Belgian Queen looks radiant in this chic suit made of silk brocade *far right*. The softly cut collar is very flattering and the deep cuffs of fur that trim the three-quarter-length sleeves add just the right amount of detail

Ermine fur trims the entire length of the dress train

THE SPANISH CONNECTION

Fabiola brought all the dignity and stately elegance of the Spanish aristocracy to Belgium when she became Baudouin's Queen in 1960. The simply cut, tailored fashions of the 'sixties complement her dark, slightly severe, beauty. Although Fabiola is most comfortable in casual clothes, more formal outfits suit her very well indeed

Popperfoto

Popperfoto

Camera Press

AP/Topham

THE PRISONER AND THE REFUGEE

WITH MOST OF WESTERN EUROPE UNDER GERMAN CONTROL, BAUDOUIN'S CAREFREE CHILDHOOD WAS BROUGHT TO AN ABRUPT END, AS THE BELGIAN ROYAL FAMILY WERE PUSHED FROM ONE SS-GUARDED FORTRESS TO ANOTHER

Above Fabiola at just four years old, in 1932. The photograph below was taken eight years later. The carefully posed family group includes all Fabiola's brothers and sisters. Alessandro, Gonzalo and Jaime stand behind Fabiola, Nieves, Annamaria and Fabiola's twin sister, Maria Teresa

AS BAUDOUIN LANGUISHED IN SAN SEBASTIAN, struggling to master the unfamiliar consonants of Spanish, he may have imagined that the language would come in useful in the future. But almost certainly the nine-year-old Prince never envisaged that it would come in useful for talking to his future Queen – Fabiola de Mora y Aragon.

Like Baudouin, Fabiola's childhood was defined by the exigencies of war and politics. But while Baudouin's war years were just beginning, those of his wife-to-be were coming to an end. The youngest of seven children – three boys and four girls – Fabiola was born on 11 June 1928. That she was of noble blood was obvious, if only for the length of her parent's names. Her father was Don Gonzalo de Mora y Fernandez, Riera del Olmo, Count of Mora and Marquess of Casa Riera; her mother was Dona Bianca de Aragon y Carillo de Albornoz, Barroeta-Aldamar y Elio. That Fabiola was the baby of the family, however, was less easily discernible: her twin sister, Maria Teresa, had taken her first breath just minutes before her own birth.

Fabiola's upbringing had been a strange combination of the luxurious and the spartan, the settled and the peripatetic. Her early days had been spent in the marble halls of Don

Camera Press

Camera Press

Meanwhile, the lights were going out across Europe. And through the darkness, homeward bound for Brussels, thundered the train carrying the children of Leopold III. With most of Western Europe firmly under the jackboot, and looking likely to stay that way for some time, tutor Gatien du Parc decided to bring his charges back to Belgium. Accordingly, on 2 August 1940, Baudouin, Albert and Josephine-Charlotte were reunited with their father.

The newly returned refugees found the King under virtual house arrest at Laeken. All visitors were screened at the gates by German sentries; Leopold was not allowed to venture outside the

'Baudouin has never

told a lie'

KING LEOPOLD

grounds without permission from his gaolers; and even inside the palace itself, German soldiers kept a vigilant eye on their prisoner. Moreover, as an ironic counterpoint, the palace was dangerously exposed to Allied air raids.

It was no place for children, and the two Princes were soon packed off to the Royal château at Ciergnon in the Ardennes. Princess Josephine-Charlotte, however, was despatched to a Brussels boarding school, the Institut de la Vierge Fidèle. Ciergnon not being within the

Gonzalo's Madrid residence, the Palace Zurbano. As befitted the home of a nobleman who was a close friend of King Alfonso XIII of Spain, the main rooms were luxuriously packed with antiques and precious paintings. By contrast, however, the bedrooms were austere.

The massive brood had a temporal overseer in the form of their governess, Milagros de Rasines. But it was the Almighty who held real power in the Palace Zurbano. Having been recently ennobled by the Vatican, the family was repaying its debt to the Church by living a life of strict piety. One firm rule, for example, was that all the palace servants remain single. And it was no coincidence that the private quarters had a tinge of monasticism.

Forced to leave Spain

But Fabiola's childhood was as overshadowed by disaster as Baudouin's. King Alfonso had never been loved by his people – his wedding, in 1906, had been marred by just the first of several assassination attempts – and when the Great Depression seized Spain, popular discontent came to a head. In 1931 Spain declared itself a Republic, and Alfonso fled the country. With him went the loyal ranks of the Mora y Aragons. Unlike the King, however, Fabiola's family were not condemned to permanent exile.

Almost as soon as they returned home, the Spanish Civil War broke out. Once again the Mora y Aragons packed their bags and joined half a million refugees streaming out of the country. By the time they finally returned, the rest of the continent was engulfed in war, and neutral Spain was licking its wounds. It was under the dictatorship of General Franco that the chandeliers shone once more in the Palace Zurbano.

♛ For much of her childhood, home for Fabiola was the Palace Zurbano in Madrid above. Fabiola received the traditional sheltered upbringing of a daughter of the Spanish aristocracy. But the 1930s were turbulent years. Civil war forced thousands to flee Spain below and the Mora y Aragons were among them – although, luckier than many, Fabiola's family were able to return

Hulton Picture Company

radius of Leopold's German leash, it was up to Baudouin and Albert to visit their father. On alternate Sundays they travelled to Laeken to spend the day with him.

That first winter at Ciergnon was bitterly cold. The temperature fell below freezing and snow covered the ground to a depth of more than three feet. Still, Baudouin was undeterred. He took the opportunity to perfect his skiing and, indoors, studied by the fireside. So that he should master the two languages spoken in his kingdom, lessons were taught in French and in Flemish on alternate days. Soon he could speak Flemish as fluently as his native French. Possibly this was due to the fact that his Flemish teacher, Monsieur Paelinck, also taught him science, the subject of which he was fondest.

Leopold's unpopularity

Leopold, meanwhile, was in disgrace throughout the free world. He was accused (unjustly, it was later proved) of surrendering the Belgian Army to the Germans without giving the Allies any prior warning, and so, at a stroke, exposing the Allied armies' left flank and means of retreat to the enemy. And then, most unwisely, he visited Hitler at Berchtesgaden. 'You can rummage in vain,' cried British politician Lloyd George, 'through the black annals of the most reprobate kings of the earth to find a blacker and more squalid sample of perfidy and poltroonery than that perpetrated by the King of the Belgians.'

As if to reinforce his point, four London spiritualists claimed to have been visited by the extremely distressed ghost of Astrid. In Paris a statue of King Albert, Leopold's father, was draped in black. It was even suggested that

Hulton Picture Company

♔ *The 13-year-old Baudouin was a keen Scout above. Amidst the turmoil of war-torn Europe, Leopold and Liliane struggled to give the children as normal an upbringing as possible. Baudouin and Albert spent much of the war in the Ardennes, at the Royal château of Ciergnon right, while Josephine-Charlotte was educated at a boarding school in Brussels*

Popperfoto

Popperfoto

Hulton Picture Company

LILIANE BAELS

Liliane Baels, the woman destined to become Baudouin's stepmother, first met King Leopold III in 1938, when she was just 22 years old. Born in London of Flemish parents, she received a thoroughly upper-class upbringing. She had been educated in the Convent of the Sacred Heart in Ostend and then at a fashionable finishing school in London. As Governor of West Flanders, her father, Henri Baels, enjoyed the use of Bruges Palace as his official residence. And in 1935 Liliane had been presented to King George V and Queen Mary at Buckingham Palace. But she was still not good enough for the Belgian people, who would not accept a commoner as their Queen. Even Liliane herself, when Leopold proposed to her, pointed out that 'kings marry princesses'. The marriage brought forth a storm of disapproval that lasted for a quarter of a century

Leopold was a German impostor called Olden-dorff, the real King having died with Astrid.

But Leopold was very much alive. Moreover, being only 40 he was beginning to feel the pinch of being a widower. On 11 September 1941 he contracted a morganatic marriage with the 25-year-old Liliane Baels, a commoner. The ceremony took place in secret, at Laeken's private chapel, the only witnesses being Leopold's mother and Liliane's father.

A new stepmother

Princess Liliane, as she was now known, swept like a breath of fresh air through Leopold's gloomy existence at Laeken. She was strikingly beautiful, strong-willed and vivacious. The children adored her and they now returned to live at Laeken. Within just three months, however, Liliane became pregnant, and the family's honeymoon period was over.

On 6 December, Leopold requested Cardinal Van Roey to have the marriage announced from every pulpit in the land. Belgium's congregations greeted the news with sour faces. 'We

👑 *Belgian troops march past the Royal Palace in Brussels on 8 April 1940 left. Only one month later, on 10 May, German forces invaded Belgium. After 18 days of fighting, the Belgian Army was overwhelmed and forced to surrender*

A Catholic Alliance

Albert I (1875-1934) m. Elisabeth of Bavaria (1876-1965)

Charles, Count of Flanders (1903-1983)

Marie-José (1906-)

Prince Carl of Sweden (1859-1953) m. Princess Ingeborg of Sweden

Lilian Baels (1916-) m.(2) Leopold III (1901-1983) m.(1) Princess Astrid of Sweden (1905-1935)

Don Gonzalo de Mora y Fernandez (d.1957) m. Dona Bianca de Aragon y Carillo

Alexandre (1942-) Marie Christine (1951-) Marie Esmeralda (1956-)

3 brothers 3 sisters

Princess Paola Ruffo di Calabria (1937-) m. Albert, Prince of Liège (1934-)

Josephine-Charlotte (1927-)

Baudouin I (1930-) m. Dona Fabiola de Mora y Aragon (1928-)

Prince Philippe (1960-) Princess Astrid (1962-) Prince Laurent (1963-)

Camera Press

other country pursuits. And there was driving – in a real car: a little Fiat that the King of Italy had given to Leopold as a wedding present. For a few years Boudouin was once more able to enjoy the pleasures of a 'normal' family life.

But as the war began to turn against Germany, so the bombs started to fall. And in May 1944, after a near miss at Laeken, Leopold decided his children would be safer back at Ciergnon. In June, the Allies landed in France and Himmler decreed that Leopold be taken to Germany. Leopold persuaded the officer in charge to stop at Ciergnon so that he could say goodbye to his children. On arrival, however, he discovered that they had just left for Brussels.

Belga

THE ROYAL PALACE

The Brussels residence of the Belgian Royal Family was built in the early part of this century by Leopold II. The avaricious Leopold had acquired the Congo Free State in 1885 and made a fortune from the colony, which he used to fund an ambitious building programme. The Palace is built on a slope; one author has described the building as looking like a piece of cake that is about to slip off a carelessly balanced plate. No expense was spared on the decoration of the interior, particularly in the Throne Room, from the ceiling of which hang several quite spectacular chandeliers

thought you had your face turned towards us in mourning,' wailed one Brussels newspaper, 'instead you had it hidden on the shoulder of a woman.'

To those who cherished the memory of Astrid, Liliane was a usurper. She now held her predecessor's title of Princesse de Rethy (but not that of Queen). To the aristocracy she was a for-tune-hunter. To patriots she was a disgrace – her father had fled to the south of France, her brother had deliberately avoided military ser-vice. To constitutionalists she wasn't even legally married, because the match lacked minis-terial sanction. And to Walloons she was simply Flemish. One government minister summed up the mood of the country when he declared: 'The people do not accept such a marriage. They accept it in a film, in a novel, in some other coun-try, or in a history book...'

For 11-year-old Baudouin, however, the arrival of Liliane opened a new chapter in his young life. For hours on end the two would play in the grounds of Laeken. There were fishing and

♛ *General de Gaulle (shown left in the photograph* right*) is cheered by the Belgian people as he rides through the streets of Brussels in October 1945. Sitting beside him is Leopold's brother Prince Charles. Before the Germans finally moved out in 1944, they had taken Leopold and his family to Germany. Charles also spent the war in the hands of the Germans, but was luckier than his brother and not deported. After the Allied landings in Normandy, he managed to escape and stay in hiding until Belgium was free again. As the most senior member of the Royal Family still in the country, he was created Regent of Belgium in September 1944*

When a well-meaning soldier offered to delay his departure until the Princes could be found, Leopold refused. 'No,' he said, 'they'll only make me cry.' And so he continued his journey to the fortress of Hirschtein, near Dresden.

If the sight of his children would have made him cry, Leopold was to be given plenty of opportunity for tears. For Liliane, Baudouin and the others were soon being driven to join him. It was a three-day journey of utter misery. Baudouin had measles, Albert had mumps, and in the minds of all the children was the memory of their flight through France at the beginning of the war. Only when they arrived at Hirschtein, on 11 June, did the ordeal seem over. In fact it was just beginning.

Imprisoned in Germany

The Royal Family's German gaolers approached their task with Teutonic thoroughness. Surrounded by a triple barrier of barbed wire and guarded by a 70-man contingent of SS soldiers complete with dogs, the tiny Belgian contingent were completely isolated from the outer world. The Governor, Lurker, ordained that only German radio be broadcast in their quarters – but by night the family would tune into the BBC on a radio that Liliane had hidden in her luggage.

Summer mellowed into autumn, which sharpened into a cruel winter. The food was poor and the cold frightful. In place of the candle-spiked Christmas trees of better times, Christmas Day saw the family huddled round a single wax stub watching despondently as the flame slowly ate its way down the wick. It was a miserable period. By the following spring, the Allies were advancing again. On 6 March the

Belgian Royal Family were told to get themselves ready for a change of residence. Their destination was a wooden chalet near Salzburg, in Austria, where they were surrounded once more by barbed wire fences and SS guards.

For Baudouin, just 14 years old, it must have been an appalling experience. Every day, as the Allies ground nearer and as the guards grew more nervous and trigger-happy, he feared a sudden and swift death. Then, on 7 May, his worst nightmares seemed on the point of realization when a group of SS soldiers came clattering into the Royal quarters. But the guards had come to surrender. The American Seventh Army was on its way. A little later, Sherman tanks rolled through the barbed wire. Baudouin and his family were now free, amid what Liliane described as 'the most beautiful mess I've ever seen'.

☙**Above** *The Belgian Royal Family at the Villa Reposoir at Prègney, near Geneva in neutral Switzerland, soon after their liberation by American troops in May 1945. Josephine-Charlotte, Baudouin and Albert are standing behind Leopold and the beautiful Liliane, who share the the sofa with their three-year-old son Alexandre. Leopold was so unpopular in Belgium, where he was accused, probably unjustly, of collaboration with the German occupying forces, that the Belgians would not allow him back into their country, and he was forced to remain an exile for another five years*

Family Album
The Belgian Royal Children

Popperfoto

♔ After the death of their mother, Queen Astrid, the Belgian children continued to spend summer holidays in Sweden, staying with Astrid's mother, Princess Carl, at her summer residence, Fridhem. *Left* Their grandmother tries to convince Albert to join his brother Baudouin and sister Josephine-Charlotte to pose for a photograph on top of a mossy mound

♔ The young Baudouin admired his father enormously and *below* he emulates the dare-devil Leopold at the wheel of a magnificent toy racing car

Popperfoto

Hulton Picture Company

Popperfoto

👑Leopold's second family, his three
children by Liliane *above right*:
Prince Alexandre with his two young
sisters, Marie Christine and, in his
arms, the one-year-old Marie
Esmeralda, who was born in 1956

👑Baudouin and Josephine-Charlotte
right with baby Albert, aged two
weeks. Albert grew up to enjoy the
same games as most boys of his age,
such as playing cowboys and
Indians in the grounds of the Royal
Palace *above*

Popperfoto

TO THE MANNER BORN

King Baudouin came to the Belgian throne at a very young age. Many of his countrymen – and probably he himself – had grave doubts about his ability to rule, but over the 40 years of his reign he has shown himself to be a conscientious and compassionate ruler, and Baudouin and his chosen Queen, Fabiola, have gained their subjects' love and respect

☙The day after his father's formal abdication, 20-year-old Baudouin takes the Oath of Allegiance before a joint session of Parliament in the Parliament Building, Brussels, on 17 July 1951 *left*. There is no actual coronation ceremony in Belgium, but the elaborate canopy surmounted by a crown helps to make the event truly regal

☙Queen Fabiola prefers the simple life, but – as befitted by her aristocratic background – when she dresses up in evening-wear and jewels, she looks every inch the queen she is. She has a tiara to suit every formal occasion: the one she is wearing *above right* was a wedding present from General Francisco Franco and the Spanish people. Of gold and platinum, it is decorated with rubies, diamonds and pearls. Fabiola wears another ruby-studded tiara in London *right*. By her side is her sister-in-law Paola

☙*Far right* For state occasions, Baudouin wears Gala Uniform: black with gold buttons and braid epaulettes. Across his chest is draped the purple Grand Cordon of the Order of Leopold, the oldest and highest Belgian order. It was instituted during the reign of Leopold I, who reigned from 1831 to 1865, and conferred on Baudouin when he became King. Baudouin also wears the eight-pointed star of the Order of the Garter, conferred on him by Queen Elizabeth in 1963

Hulton Picture Company

Camera Press

Popperfoto

Hulton Picture Company

OUT OF THE BLUE

KING IN NAME ONLY, BAUDOUIN WAS IGNORED BY THE MAJORITY OF HIS SUBJECTS UNTIL HE ASTONISHED THEM WITH THE ANNOUNCEMENT OF HIS ENGAGEMENT TO FABIOLA

BAUDOUIN AND HIS FAMILY WERE NOW FREE. But Liberation did not mean that they could return to Belgium. The Belgian Government refused to let a 'traitor King' resume his throne. Instead they decided that Leopold's brother Charles, who had been hiding underground with the Belgian resistance movement, the *maquis* – and who had been looking forward to a quiet post-war existence – should act as Regent. The Prime Minister, Paul Henri Spaak, informed Leopold, 'We cannot say with you "Long live the King," but ... I am ready to say "Sire, your son is our King."'

Exile in Switzerland

Undeterred, if not unaffected, by events at home, Leopold and his family settled by the shores of Lake Geneva in the villa *Le Reposoir*. It was an old, comfortable house, with well-tended lawns that sloped down to the lake and, on fine days, a distant view of Mont Blanc. Visitors were struck by what a happy family group they made. Liliane, by now 'a beautiful woman of twenty eight, with dark hair and luminous eyes, a matt-white complexion and a willowy, sinuous figure', was the life and soul of the party, keeping everyone amused with her witty conversation and after-dinner charades.

Prince Baudouin was a tall, bespectacled youth who retained all the gravity of his childhood. A student at the College of Geneva, he took his work seriously. Every morning he would rise early and walk to his classes, or sometimes take the tram, always travelling third class. It was said that his work took precedence over everything, even rest and play.

And so it continued for five years, the only break coming in 1949, when Baudouin accompanied Leopold and Liliane on a trip to the United States. The following year, however, matters came to a head when, on 12 March 1950, some five-and-a-half million Belgians voted in a referendum to see whether Leopold should be

allowed to resume his throne. Over 57 per cent of the population declared that he should, and Leopold made ready to return home.

Belgium was torn in two. Despite the result of the referendum, there were still many, especially among the French-speaking Walloons, who did not want to see their former King take up his position again. And they made their feelings very clear. There were anti-Leopold demonstrations at Antwerp, Ghent, Mons and Namur. On 14 July, a mob of 10,000 assembled in

♔ *When, in July 1951, Baudouin took his solemn oath of allegiance, the crowds in the streets of Brussels were unanimous in their support* far left. *Things had not run so smoothly for the young Prince* above left *in the difficult post-war years, matters coming to a head with the controversial return of King Leopold from Switzerland in 1950* below

Popperfoto

Topham

Jack Esten/Camera Press

La Louvière, crying, 'Hang him, Hang him!' And Spaak sent an open letter to the King, begging him to reconsider. He offered what seemed a reasonable solution: 'May you send us your son.'

Leopold did send them his son. But he came too. At 7.15 on the morning of 22 July, Leopold, accompanied by Prince Albert and the 19-year-old Baudouin, flew into Brussels. Less than 300 people waited to see the Royal arrivals bundled into a car and then, escorted by four armoured cars, driven through the empty streets to Laeken. As the heavily guarded gates shut behind them, Leopold must have been reminded of a similar imprisonment just ten years earlier.

A country in uproar

On 27 July, thousands of demonstrators, shouting 'Leopold to the gallows!' clashed with a group of loyalists outside Laeken. Paving stones began to fly, and it took a charge by sabre-wielding mounted police to clear the area. By 30 July, the entire eastern half of Belgium was paralyzed by strikes. When police killed three demonstrators near Liège, the situation escalated. As 100,000 demonstrators marched on Brussels, the country teetered on the brink of civil war. The following afternoon Leopold was met by a government deputation demanding his resignation.

WARTIME ROYALTY

World War 2 was a turbulent time for Europe's monarchies. Although offered asylum by Britain, Leopold of Belgium chose to stay with his family and countrymen. King Christian of Denmark did the same, but while Leopold was criticized by the allies, Christian won approval by openly wearing the yellow star which the Nazis forced his Jewish citizens to wear.

Others, however, fled their countries. The rulers of Greece, Yugoslavia, Luxemburg, Norway and the Netherlands all took refuge abroad. Sometimes their escapes were dramatic: Queen Wilhelmina of the Netherlands was spirited away in a British warship two days after her country was invaded; and King George II of Greece got out at the last minute in an RAF Sunderland flying boat. But few had such an arduous odyssey as King Zog of Albania. When Italy invaded his realm on 7 April 1939, he fled – with his three-day-old son and the crown jewels – in a cavalcade of enormous motor cars. It was not until the following June that the Royal caravan reached northern France, only days ahead of the German forces.

Not all were so lucky. Princess Mafalda of Italy died in Buchenwald concentration camp. Crown Princess Antoinette of Bavaria also went to Buchenwald, where she was severly tortured. Although she survived the war, the injuries she had received were so damaging that she died prematurely in 1954

On 12 August 1950, at a joint session of the Belgian Parliament, Prince Baudouin swore to give himself entirely to his country right. Even though his father had abdicated, the troubled Royal Family was still able to relax together in the grounds of Laeken. Gathered around Albert at the wheel of his car above are (from left to right) Baudouin, Liliane, Alexandre and Leopold

Topham

' *My dear father...I promise I will do everything in my power to prove myself worthy to be your son* '

BAUDOUIN AT HIS CORONATION

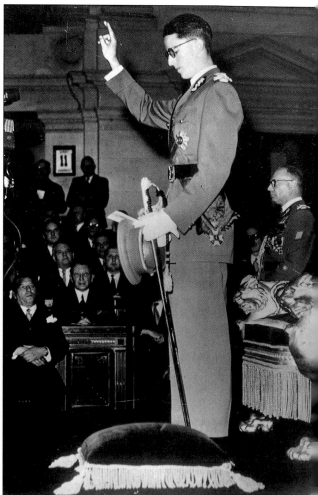

Hulton Picture Company

The young King was subjected to vicious attacks in the press when, in February 1953, much of Belgium suffered from catastrophic flooding. At the time Baudouin was on holiday with his father and stepmother in Nice. When he became aware of the hostility brewing back home, Baudouin returned and toured the flooded areas left, but the resentment felt by many who had suffered in the disaster took a long time to disappear

PRINCE ROYAL

By 8.00 pm on 31 July Leopold had agreed to his government's demands. Power would devolve to Baudouin, who would become Prince Royal until his 21st birthday, when he would be allowed to ascend the throne. At dawn on 1 August, the message was read to the press. Ten days later, Baudouin was elevated to the rank of Lieutenant General, the highest rank in the Belgian army, and the following day, wearing his stiff new uniform, he took his oath of office.

The first years were hard. Although Baudouin took his constitutional oath as sovereign on 17 July 1951, many felt that it was Leopold who still ruled. The ex-King still lived in his suite at Laeken, for instance, while Baudouin remained in his old childhood quarters. And at mealtimes, it was Leopold who sat at the head of the table, not Baudouin. When he became King, Baudouin had declared, 'My dear father ... I promise that I will do everything in my power to prove myself worthy to be your son.'

Though it was now the initial 'B' that surmounted the emblem of the Belgian crown, the initial 'L' lurked behind like a heavy watermark. Determined that the insults paid to his father during the war should not be forgotten, he refused to attend the funeral of Britain's King George VI in 1952. And he likewise refused to have any dealings with those who had stood against Leopold on his return from Switzerland.

The shadow of war

Once again all the rumours of wartime resurfaced, and people began to blame Liliane. Baseless attacks, which infuriated Baudouin, were launched at her by the press. On one occasion he was reported to have flung the newspaper to the ground and left the room. When he returned he

MARIE-JOSÉ

With Leopold an unwilling King in exile, the last of King Albert's three children was about to become the unwanted Queen of Italy. In 1930, Baudouin's aunt, Marie-José, had married the heir to the Italian throne, Crown Prince Umberto. It was a bad match. The Belgian Princess was a serious, cultured lady, Umberto a pleasure-seeking womanizer. When Marie-José's train came off on her wedding day, it was reckoned to be an omen of a doomed alliance. King Victor Emmanuel abdicated in favour of Umberto on 9 May 1946, but the monarchy's popularity was at a low ebb. In a referendum held on 3 June, the Italians voted by 12 to 10 million for a republic. Two days after, Marie-José and her four children left for Portugal, later to be joined by Umberto. Their reign as King and Queen of Italy had lasted just 25 days

Popperfoto

Popperfoto

When Leopold's sons' thoughts turned to marriage, it was the wrong son who was the first to wed. Many Belgians would have loved to welcome the glamorous Princess Paola as their Queen, but she was to marry Baudouin's younger brother Albert. Nevertheless, the first official picture of Albert and Paola together left did a lot of good for public morale and brought the Belgian Royal Family to the attention of the world's press

♛ *The young King of the Belgians took his duties seriously, doing his best to remain on good terms with neighbouring countries such as Holland and Germany. On a visit to Germany in 1959 he made a tour of inspection of Belgian troops stationed at Düren* left. *The following year he proved a gracious escort to Princess Beatrix of the Netherlands* below, *when she accompanied her mother Queen Juliana on a state visit to Belgium*

ELISABETH

While King Baudouin remained unmarried, it was his grandmother Elisabeth who held sway as Belgium's Queen. A diminutive but dynamic figure, whose motto in life seemed to be 'I always do what I wish', Elisabeth achieved enormous popularity for her patronage of medicine and the arts. But what endeared her most to the Belgians was her wilful eccentricity. She was a fitness fanatic who, even in her eighties, took cold baths, went swimming, took long walks and did yoga exercises every day. When she learned that one luncheon guest was also interested in yoga, she insisted he drop his knife and fork and practise breathing control with her. She was fascinated by birds, and could be found creeping round the park at Laeken with a microphone to record their song. She was also a passionate musician. When discovered at six in the morning playing her violin at the bottom of a bomb crater, she exclaimed, 'It's such a lovely morning, and the acoustics in this crater are perfect.' On another occasion she sat out the whole night playing Brahms and Schubert quartets in the middle of a golf course.

After her death in 1965, at the age of 89, an exhibition of her possessions neatly catalogued her varied life. There was a miner's lamp from 1903, Egyptian jewellery from her opening of Tutankhamen's tomb in 1923, a 5000-year-old clay tablet from Ur, two figurines of the Emperor and Empress of Japan, a bust she had made of her gardener and the Croix de Mérite of the Rumanian Air Force

cancelled all official appointments for that day. 'I don't know how that boy can carry on,' remarked one observer.

In 1953, floods swept over Belgium, Holland and Britain. But while the Dutch and British Royals rushed to the disaster areas, Baudouin was on the Riviera acquiring a tan with his father and stepmother. He did in fact return to Belgium, but immediately contracted influenza and returned to the Riviera. The unfortunate Liliane, it was decided, must be to blame for his callousness.

Then in 1959, Baudouin announced that his younger brother Albert was to marry the Italian Princess Paola Ruffo di Calabria. The Belgians

24

Belga

♛ *The picture that emerged of the mysterious Fabiola was of a fairly timid and reserved young woman* left. *But she showed that she was able to let her hair down on occasion, for example, when she was being serenaded* below *by a group of grim-faced students at the University of Madrid*

always be looked upon as merely 'the son of Leopold III'.

The Belgians echoed that sentiment whole-heartedly. They looked at Albert and saw him with his glamorous Italian wife. They looked at Josephine-Charlotte and saw her by the side of Prince Jean of Luxemburg, who she had married in 1953. But when they looked at Baudouin they saw a solitary, bespectacled figure peering shyly out from a plain, rather baggy, suit. There were even some who sarcastically cried 'Vive la Reine!' whenever his sister-in-law, Princess Paola, went by. There were even rumours that *Le Roi Triste*, as they called Baudouin, intended to abdicate in favour of his brother Albert and become a Trappist monk.

On 16 September 1960, the populace was therefore delighted when the Prime Minister, Gaston Eyskens, made a broadcast to the nation, announcing that the King was engaged to be

were outraged, not only because Baudouin had failed to consult the government, but also because the marriage was to be held in the Vatican and not in Belgium. It was hastily arranged that the ceremony take place in Brussels, but resentment simmered on. And Liliane, it was said, had orchestrated the whole thing.

Eventually, however, Leopold and Liliane bowed to public pressure and left Laeken for a

'I really feel he is the only man in the world that I could love for ever'

FABIOLA TO PILAR DE SASTAGO

private residence just outside Brussels. Here they quietly faded from public view, Leopold devoting most of his time to entomology and making frequent trips to the tropics from where he would bring back specimens for the Brussels Natural History Museum.

What really worried the press and the Belgian public was that Baudouin was still single. No less than 24 suitable fiancées – including Princess Margaret – had been suggested in the papers, but nothing had come of them. Even Baudouin's grandmother, Elisabeth, pointed out that he would never truly become Baudouin I until he married. As a bachelor King he would

married to Dona Fabiola de Mora y Aragon. Throughout the country, atlases were flattened down at the map marked *Espagne*. Who was this woman from a far country who had won the heart of their bachelor King?

Now in her early thirties, Fabiola had matured into a shy, pious lady whose private education by a tutor had left her with an abiding fondness for music and art. She had had plenty of hands-on experience of life, having trained as a nurse in the Spanish Army and worked in a Madrid hospital. And she had travelled widely, becoming fluent in English, German and French.

She remained, however, a retiring person. Her main concern in life was to help children, to which end she had written a book of nursery stories, *The Twelve Marvellous Tales*, the royalties from which were given to children's charities. Authorship apart, she liked to keep herself and

Popperfoto

♔ *Baudouin gave his fiancée a shy but tender greeting above when she landed at Brussels airport on 20 October 1960. The political problems of Belgium were weighing heavily on his shoulders; the Government had just announced the closure of 11 coal mines in the south of the country and angry miners had flocked to the capital to protest*

♔ *With the threat of thousands of coal-miners marching on the capital to ruin the Royal wedding day, security was much in evidence when the King and Fabiola were driven round the working-class districts of Brussels right to allow the people a glimpse of their future Queen. Those in the crowd who could get close enough showered the couple with flowers and confetti*

her family out of the limelight. But in this desire she was thwarted by the behaviour of her elder brother Jaime, who loved publicity as much as she shunned it.

Just a year or two older than Fabiola, Jaime was the black sheep of the family. His playboy lifestyle and bohemian existence were an endless source of fascination for the world's gossip columns, and a constant source of irritation for Fabiola. She considered him to be a disgrace to the family name. He, on the other hand, declared that he was the 'glory' of the family because he was the only one who worked – though his jobs, which ranged from nightclub pianist to a reputed two years in the French Foreign Legion, did little to impress his sister. Their mother, Dona Bianca, was constantly having to patch up the rows that broke out between the two. In 1957, the fights stopped for a time as the family

Loomis Dean/Camera Press

Belga

united to mourn the death of the elderly Marquess. But the gloom of Fabiola's bereavement was unexpectedly dispelled by love.

How Baudouin and Fabiola first met remains a closely guarded secret. When questioned by the press in 1960, the smiling Belgian monarch replied, 'We're keeping that story for our children.' All that the Palace would admit was that 'The King met Señorita Fabiola several times with friends during various travels.' One spokesman, throwing caution to the winds, announced that three years before, in the year that Don Gonzalo died, Baudouin had spent a holiday in Spain where he had acquired 'some elements of the Spanish language'.

True love

But it seems likely that he picked up more than just a smattering of the language on his visit to Spain. It was probably then that Fabiola is said to have confided to her closest friend, Pilar de Sastago, 'Today, I have just spent two wonderful hours, two hours with a man I could happily adore. I really feel he is the only man in the world that I could love for ever.'

👑 *Baudouin introduced Fabiola officially to the Belgian and international press on 19 September 1960. The photo session above took place on the steps of the Royal hunting lodge at Ciergnon in the Ardennes, which had been decked out specially with huge bunches of pink and white flowers. Baudouin was rather nervous and awkward in front of the cameras, but he was obviously delighted to be reunited with his fiancée and no doubt confident that Fabiola would be a great comfort and support through the looming political crisis*

LAEKEN PALACE

Built in the late 18th century for Marie-Christine of Austria and her husband Prince Albert of Saxony, Laeken Palace went down in history in 1802 when Napoleon signed the order there for his armies to advance into Russia. After a devastating fire in 1890, it had to be rebuilt. Situated in the suburbs of Brussels, Laeken Palace is today King Baudouin and Queen Fabiola's private residence and is famous for its vast park and its magnificent hot-houses

Belga

♛*Above* The back of the Palace features a large rotunda with a cupola constructed of metal, and contrasts with the austere and temple-like main entrance of the building *right*. The centre part of the Palace was reduced to a gutted shell after the fire in 1890 but the original style of the façade was closely adhered to when the reconstruction works were carried out. The Palace and Estate of Laeken as we know it today was created by Leopold II (1835-1909), who not only restored and rebuilt the Palace but also enlarged it, doubled the size of the Estate and had broad avenues laid all around it. Historically, the Royal Estate of Laeken dates back to the late 18th century, when the provinces of what constitutes Belgium today were under Austrian rule. After the Austrian era, Laeken became the residence of Napoleon and his wife, Empress Josephine, and later of King William of the Netherlands. Since Belgian Independence in 1830, the Palace has been the home of the Belgian Royal Family

Belga

Belga

♛ *Left and below* In 1876 Leopold II had a group of greenhouses built onto the existing Orangery dating from the Dutch period. Fourteen years later, he commissioned a second group of greenhouses, and it was his wish that the Royal Greenhouses, as they became known, should be opened to the public every year for a few weeks in spring − a custom which is still respected by the present Royal Family. The greenhouses boast a superb collection of exotic plants and flowers − the annual display of hundreds of different azalea species is particularly spectacular, and the palm tree collection has been likened to the famous Palm House at Kew Gardens. The remarkable metal structure of the arches is repeated in most of the greenhouses. Supported by cast-iron pillars, they are attractively decorated with motifs in wrought iron

Belga

Camera Press

♛ Behind the scenes: King Baudouin and Queen Fabiola relax in the drawing-room of the Palace with their two dogs *left*. However, their respective duties often extend beyond the working day well into the evening, and Queen Fabiola had to set up a secretariat at Laeken to handle all the correspondence for her charity and welfare work. Many interior alterations in the Palace reflect the Queen's excellent taste and her expert knowledge of period furniture

Hulton Picture Company

THE SAD KING SMILES

DESPITE THE POLITICAL AND ECONOMIC PROBLEMS THAT BESET THE COUNTRY, THE PEOPLE WARMED TO THE OBVIOUS HAPPINESS OF BAUDOUIN AND HIS BRIDE

👑 *At the pre-wedding banquet, which was given by the Belgian Government in honour of the bride and groom, Fabiola and Baudouin had appeared a little apprehensive above. Fabiola was wearing the tiara she had been presented by Dona Carmen, the wife of General Franco, in the name of the people of Spain below*

I T WAS THE PERIOD IN WHICH HAROLD Macmillan claimed, 'You've never had it so good.' His words may have held true for Britain, but Belgium was bitterly divided over educational reforms, it had just lost its colony of the Congo, and there was heavy unemployment. Accordingly the wedding of their King, which was set for 15 December 1960, provided a welcome ray of sunshine.

On 6 December, Baudouin arrived at the airport to escort Fabiola off the plane, and the country began to gear itself up for the celebrations. Baudouin and Fabiola had already exchanged engagement presents. He sent her an emerald ring; she gave him a pair of diamond cufflinks. But these were nothing compared to the gifts that poured in from round the world. General Franco's wife was all smiles as she presented Fabiola with a magnificent tiara, and Britain's Queen Elizabeth sent an antique bracket clock, encased in cream lacquer and decorated with flowers.

Fabiola made sure they were not the only beneficiaries. When a commemorative wedding

Hulton Picture Company

Popperfoto

medallion was issued, all the proceeds went to a Brussels nursing school. And when they received a cheque from the nation for 9,800,000 francs (about £70,000), Baudouin immediately earmarked it as the first deposit in a 'social assistance fund for poor people'.

With the presents came the guests. Kings, queens and representatives of all Europe's monarchies began to land at Brussels airport. When Princess Margaret and Tony Armstrong-Jones

👑 *Fabiola, encouraged to step into the limelight by her husband, raises her hands to the cheering crowds from the steps of the church after the marriage ceremony right. Among the glittering array of guests gathered in Brussels were the recently married Princess Margaret and Antony Armstrong-Jones above, seen here arriving for the gala banquet on the eve of the wedding*

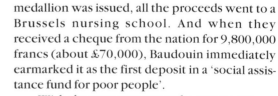

who had arrived in the throne room of the Royal Palace for the first stage in the ceremony. By 9.00 am the room, resplendent with brilliant chandeliers, scarlet wall-hangings and grey and gilt decorations, was beginning to fill up. Shortly before 10 o'clock, the reigning sovereigns arrived. At the head of the procession were the King of Norway and the Queen of the Netherlands. Princess Margaret, who had come as Queen Elizabeth's representative, struck a glamorous note in a dress of apricot-coloured silk and a matching toque hat of cock feathers. In the centre of the room, the Chief Burgomaster of Brussels sat with two aldermen at a white marble table, ready to conduct the civil rites of marriage.

Then, when all were assembled, the Royal couple made their entrance. Baudouin was dressed simply in his army uniform. Fabiola, who had already thrown back her veil to reveal the Spanish coronet, wore a boat-necked dress of

arrived the photographers were thrown into such a frenzy of excitement that they had to be expelled from the tarmac. The only notable absentees were Leopold's brother, Prince Charles, and Fabiola's brother Jaime. She had warned the latter not to leave Spain until after the wedding.

Many of the visiting dignitaries had never met Fabiola before. But when they did, at a pre-wedding banquet and ball held in the throne room of the Royal Palace, they were not disappointed. Belgium's Queen-to-be appeared radiant in a golden gown with a silk cape and, above her auburn hair, the diamond-studded coronet given to her by Spain. 'I am convinced, my dear Baudouin,' said ex-King Leopold, 'that you could not have made a better choice... She will be an attentive, devoted, loving and courageous wife, a loyal and vigilant guardian of the home in which the dynasty will be perpetuated.'

Muted enthusiasm

Meanwhile preparations were under way for the wedding itself. The streets were lined with flags, the vertical black, yellow and red stripes of Belgium alternating with the horizontal red, gold and red of Spain. Pragmatic shopkeepers decided their decorations could do double-duty for Christmas and decked their windows with a curious combination of crowns and candles.

The wedding day dawned grey and cold. And although the first spectators had arrived to line the route of the Royal procession at first light, their numbers did not swell dramatically as the morning went on. Indeed, nowhere were the crowds more than three or four deep.

None of this made any difference to those

The civil marriage top, even though it was held beneath a blaze of chandeliers in the Royal Palace, was a relatively low-key affair compared to the solemn religious ceremony that followed in the church of St Michael and St Gudule above. As they knelt before the altar, Baudouin kept a bottle of smelling salts concealed in his glove just in case Fabiola should be overwhelmed by the occasion and start to feel faint

ivory satin, trimmed with ermine.

The ceremony, which was read in both French and Flemish, and which was virtually identical to an ordinary Belgian civil marriage, took only quarter of an hour – less time than it took for the many honorary witnesses to sign their names in the register. At its conclusion, Baudouin and Fabiola remained seated at the table, chatting and laughing together, as the string of guests drove off at walking pace for the Church of St Michael and St Gudule, where the second part of the wedding would take place.

By 12.15, when Baudouin and Fabiola set out from the Palace, Brussels had been transformed. Thousands of Belgians, who had prudently kept

Toptan

in the warm until the last minute, now packed the streets, climbing lamp-posts and raising periscopes to get a better view.

As cannonades thundered from the nearby park, the Royal car appeared, garlanded with flowers. Before and behind trotted formations of lancers, magnificent in their bearskins and scarlet tunics, while the military bands that lined the route gave blasts on their silver trumpets to warn of the Royal couple's approach.

Public pomp and private joy

Through the splendour there shone one unmistakeable fact – *Le Roi Triste* was smiling at last. As *The Times* reported, 'There was no mistaking King Baudouin's happiness today as time and time again he smiled at his bride, or enjoyed some private joke with her, holding her arm perhaps a little more tightly than the rules of ceremony demanded.'

The service was full of personal touches. When they arrived at the church, Baudouin

♛ *The guard of honour* left *formed their archway of swords in the aisle of the church. After the stress of the ceremonies Baudouin and Fabiola* below *were in relaxed mood for the official photographs*

Belga

Hulton Picture Company

sniffs from Baudouin's glove, but all traces of nervousness vanished when the time came to make her responses, which she did in clear French, with scarcely a hint of accent.

After the exchange of rings, the completion of the wedding ceremony and a nuptial mass, Baudouin and Fabiola re-emerged to the rousing sound of Handel's *Hallelujah Chorus* and stood on the steps of the church to acknowledge the loud cheers of the crowd.

Discriminating crowds

Then they drove off once more through the narrow streets of Brussels. The crowds cheered the Royal couple resoundingly, but peered at the cars that followed and only applauded if the occupants met with their approval. Few would have disagreed with the words of one reporter who wrote, 'The dominant recollection from today is of the King and Queen, both obviously, almost embarrassedly happy, and both of them people in their own right.'

At the airport a Belgian military aircraft was waiting to carry the couple to their honeymoon destination: Spain. But before they left, Baudouin and Fabiola addressed the nation on television. 'I believe we understood and loved each other from our first meeting,' said Fabiola. They landed at Seville late that night and were driven to a large estate in the mountainous countryside of Cordoba, belonging to Fabiola's

> ***'I am convinced, my dear Baudouin, that you could not have made a better choice...She will be an attentive, loving and courageous wife...'***
>
> LEOPOLD TO BAUDOUIN

♛ An open-topped car was out of the question in mid-December with the possibility of snow, so the Royal couple rode in a specially designed car with a transparent roof top. Fabiola frequently flung her arms wide in a gesture of embrace right, as if she wanted to be accepted by her new people. The honeymoon destination was near the ancient city of Cordoba in southern Spain far right

himself led Fabiola up the steps. Although against all tradition, this was one area where Baudouin had insisted on having his own way. Onlookers were touched to see that their King carried a glove in which he had secreted a bottle of smelling salts for Fabiola's use.

The marriage service started with a message from the Pope. The ceremony was conducted by Cardinal Van Roey, the same man who had, so many years before, married Leopold and Astrid, and who was by now so old that he had to remain seated most of the time. Fabiola remained seated too, with her eyes cast down, taking surreptitious

Hulton Picture Company

uncle, the Marquis of Salinas.

The glory of a Royal wedding had only temporarily distracted Belgians from their economic woes. Three days after Baudouin and Fabiola set out on their honeymoon, a general strike was declared, and workers clashed daily with the police. As the Government tried to push through its programme of austerity, strikers' placards pointed out the huge cost of the Royal wedding. A cinema showing a newsreel of the wedding was stoned and looted.

By the night of 28 December a military aircraft was standing by at Seville airport. And the next day, at 6.05 pm, Baudouin and Fabiola landed back in Brussels. They were met by no great government fanfare, just a small group of staff from the palace. It was a tense time. Not until late January did the troubles simmer down. But even then, it was uncertain how high the monarchy's standing was among the people. On 29 January, the Royal couple were due to appear at a performance in Brussels' Theatre Royal. Baudouin and his advisers were in favour of cancelling the engagement – Fabiola, however, insisted that they attend.

Baudouin's fears were baseless. When they arrived they were mobbed by crowds shouting 'Vive le Roi! Vive La Reine!' It was clear to all that, on their first public appearance since their marriage, Belgian's Royal newlyweds had more than passed muster.

INDEPENDENCE FOR THE CONGO

Baudouin had planned to announce his engagement much earlier, but was delayed by momentous events in the Congo. Carved out of Africa by Henry Stanley in 1885 as the personal fiefdom of King Leopold II, the Belgian Congo was one of the least liberated of all European colonies. Granting the colony's independence in 1960 was one of Baudouin's most significant political acts. The year before he had gone on an extensive fact-finding tour of the Congo *right*. While the Africans warmed to him as a man, the Premier, Patrice Lumumba, replied to Baudouin's paternalistic speech at the independence ceremony with the words, 'We are no longer your monkeys.' Six days later the army mutinied, throwing the country into chaos and civil war.

For three years, UN forces struggled to keep the peace, amid horrifying stories of rape, murder and torture. When the UN admitted defeat, the Congo became a magnet for white mercenaries. In 1971, when the country was renamed Zaire, it was still piecing together the wreckage left by years of strife

Topham

Spectrum

PEACE AND PROSPERITY

Baudouin and Fabiola's marriage has stood the test of time and transcended the underlying sadness of their being unable to have children. Only occasionally hitting the headlines, they have worked hard for the welfare of their people and have done much to erase the memories of the 1940s and '50s, when the Belgian Royal Family's stock was at its lowest

Hulton Picture Company

♛A more permanent memory of the period of the Royal wedding is a bust of Fabiola made by Spanish sculptor Ramon Mateu. She posed for him *above* in his Madrid studio shortly before the wedding

♛This shop window decoration *left* was created to mark the happy day in December 1960 when Baudouin and Fabiola finally married, after keeping their intentions hidden from the world for so long. Among the flowers are arranged the couple's portrait, a bridal veil and a shield bearing the Royal emblem of a lion rampant

♛On holiday in Greece in 1964, Baudouin and Fabiola visited the ruined temple of Poseidon *right* on Cape Sounion, southeast of Athens

Popperfoto

During their summer holiday on the French Riviera in 1969, Baudouin devoted much of his time and energy to teaching Fabiola to swim *above*. As a couple, they have always enjoyed moments of relaxation away from the public gaze, but they have never allowed private considerations to interfere with their Royal duties. Among the many splendid gifts received by Baudouin and Fabiola at their wedding was this Louis XVI clock *right* from Prince Rainier and Princess Grace of Monaco. The allegorical theme portrayed in the gilt bronze figures is 'Peace bringing abundance and developing progress', an appropriate motto for the King and Queen of the Belgians

A PERFECT COUPLE

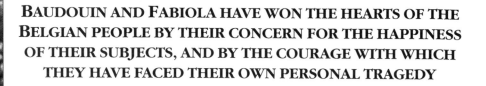

BAUDOUIN AND FABIOLA HAVE WON THE HEARTS OF THE BELGIAN PEOPLE BY THEIR CONCERN FOR THE HAPPINESS OF THEIR SUBJECTS, AND BY THE COURAGE WITH WHICH THEY HAVE FACED THEIR OWN PERSONAL TRAGEDY

Left On holiday in Spain in August 1961, a few months after Fabiola's first miscarriage, the Belgian King and Queen stroll through the woods near their holiday villa. Baudouin passed the time fishing while Fabiola took the opportunity to visit relatives and old friends

Coburg King and his wife.

On 8 June 1961, the Royal couple paid a visit to the Vatican. The press were interested to see that Fabiola was allowed to use the private Papal Elevator. It was, as a Vatican official explained, a special concession granted to her as an expectant mother. The official hastily tried to withdraw the statement, but it was too late. The news was out. The Belgians, hiding their annoyance that the announcement had been made in the Vatican rather than in Brussels, were delighted. The Sad King, it seemed, was full of surprises.

THE NEWS IN *THE TIMES* ON 18 MARCH 1961 offered a tantalizing selection of titbits: in Bangkok, the Thai Government had optimistically announced the banning of prostitution; at Nuremberg, an SS officer had been given three years' hard labour for whipping a concentration camp inmate to death; in East Berlin, a 60-year-old man had been given a slightly less severe sentence for trying to form a society for the prevention of cruelty to animals; and in Upper Darby, Pennsylvania, Mrs Arlene Cutaiar had given birth to quads. Amid this curious selection was a small notice announcing that a train had arrived in Seville to carry the King and Queen of Belgium back to Brussels after the completion of their interrupted honeymoon.

It was ironic that Baudouin and Fabiola should appear in the same spread of news as the fruitful Mrs Cutaiar. For the next decade was to be one of childless disappointment for the

'She has a charming simplicity, a kind of subdued gaiety beneath a face that is rather sad in repose, that is enormously attractive'

WILLIAM HICKEY ON FABIOLA

The Belgian press settled down to make the most of their Queen's first pregnancy. They announced that a trip to Britain, scheduled for July, would be postponed owing to Fabiola's condition. But that was about all the hard coverage they got. On 25 June, a bulletin from the Royal Palace warned that 'a happy event should not be expected'. Fabiola had suffered a miscarriage.

The rumours began again the following year. Fabiola had been to a Swiss gynaecologist; she bought clothes while she was there. A baby was expected in the following spring. But for a second time, a brief communiqué announced that Fabiola no longer expected a child.

State visit to Britain

Despite the double tragedy, Baudouin and Fabiola carried on as normal. In May 1963 Baudouin and Fabiola made a three-day state visit to London. A warm relationship rapidly developed between the two Royal Families. Banquets were held, congratulatory speeches were delivered, orders were exchanged, and so were presents. Baudouin received a 12-bore shotgun, and Fabiola was presented with a Regency rosewood table. Among the gifts given in return were a lace shawl for Queen Elizabeth, and a miniature barrel organ for Prince Andrew.

The British people, meanwhile, always concerned lest visiting royalty somehow upstage

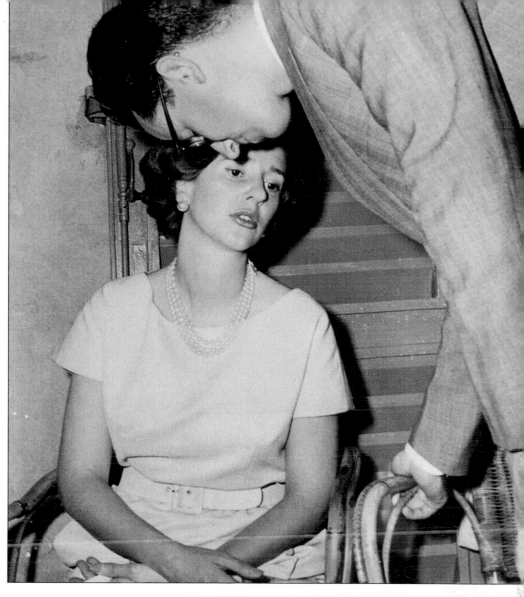

Topham

Popperfoto

Hilton Picture Company

♛Left *Baudouin and Fabiola enjoy a night at the opera with Queen Elizabeth and Prince Philip at Covent Garden Opera House in London. The Belgian Royal couple's three-day visit to Britain in May 1963 was a great success, and the rift that had existed between the two families since the war was finally closed*

♛Right *Baudouin, Pope John XXIII and Fabiola in the throne room of the Vatican. Both Baudouin and Fabiola took their religion very seriously. It was a major event in their lives when, in June 1961, they were granted a private audience with the Pope. Fabiola was permitted to wear white, a privilege of all Roman Catholic sovereigns. (Britain's Queen Elizabeth has to wear black when she visits the Vatican.) By the following day the pregnant Queen was feeling the strain top. During a reception at the Belgian embassy in Rome, her exhaustion is obvious*

39

Topham

Hulton Picture Company

👑 *The young King and Queen go about their business as modern constitutional monarchs. Clad in waders, Baudouin visits flood victims in southern Belgium above left. And above Baudouin and Fabiola set off for a helicopter flight over the port of Antwerp*

👑 Left *Queen Fabiola cuddles a baby, but, alas, not her own. The child was one of the 70 hostages released by Congolese guerillas in November 1964. The King and Queen were at Brussels airport to welcome the hostages, who had suffered beatings and forced marches at the hands of their captors, as they returned to Belgium*

Popperfoto

their own, found Baudouin and Fabiola perfect guests. By the time the Royal couple attended a ballet at Covent Garden, they had become firm favourites. One newspaper reporter, who wrote of 'a splendid flowering of improbable-looking foreign orders, some of which might well have been designed by colour-blind potentates suffering from a surfeit of arak,' noted with approval that Baudouin bore just two modest stars on his tail-coat. Even the gossip columnist William Hickey found kind words for the Belgian Queen: 'She has a charming simplicity, a kind of subdued gaiety beneath a face that is rather sad in repose, that is enormously attractive.'

Crossed fingers in Belgium

The sadness was not about to go away. In the late summer of 1963, Fabiola and Baudouin took a seaside holiday in northern Spain, not far from San Sebastian. On 22 August, just two months after Fabiola's 35th birthday, there came a court communiqué. 'The King will return alone from holiday. Although the Queen is in excellent health, she has been advised against taking long

THE PLAYBOY BROTHER

In 1966 Baudouin's brother-in-law, Jaime de Mora y Aragon, decided to write his autobiography, *Me* – subtitled 'Memoirs of a 20th-century Don Quixote'. Though the book never appeared, the title fitted Fabiola's flamboyant playboy brother down to the ground. 'I have a great deal of affection for my sister. In fact, she's always been my favourite,' Jaime once claimed in a hurt voice when questioned about his relationship with Fabiola.

The Belgian Queen, however, had different ideas. Appearing on occasions like a cross between Tommy Cooper and Salvador Dali, with exaggerated moustache, monocle, flowing robes and fez, Jaime was not Fabiola's idea of a respectable relative. His many and varied occupations had included being an actor, songwriter, singer, musician, producer of television commercials and owner of fashionable clubs. Every time Fabiola saw his picture in the papers – invariably at a nightclub, and usually playing the piano with a bottle of whisky perched on the top – she would shudder.

Jaime, however, found Fabiola's coolness puzzling. 'My sister won't receive me at her palace because I advertise shirts. But I've just learnt that another member of the Spanish aristocracy has just signed a contract to do a brand of beer for half the price I'm asking for. It's people like that who really spoil your job'

Belza

Popperfoto

journeys for the present.' Every mother could read between the lines

The collective fingers of Belgium were crossed. Throughout the country people flocked to pray for their Queen. And Baudouin himself drove to Lourdes in the hope of interceding between the House of Coburg and the House of God. It was in vain. Twenty-five days later there came the – by now – familiar announcement. Fabiola had suffered another miscarriage. The

👑 *Fabiola talks to a young boy above at the Queen Fabiola Home for Handicapped Children. The Queen has made the needs of the nation's youth her area of special interest and regularly visits hospitals and children's homes. So great is her workload that she has her own secretariat at Laeken to handle all her calls and correspondence*

nation grieved for her. A young shop assistant in Brussels was quoted as saying, 'With Fabiola there is always hope. She is the bravest woman in Belgium. God will make her a mother.'

For the moment, however, it looked as if Fabiola had decided to give childbearing a rest, and flung herself wholeheartedly into the arduous job of being Queen. Since her arrival at Laeken, Fabiola had put her distinctive stamp on Belgian Royal life. For the first time in the country's history, Belguim had a Queen who refused to have a lady-in-waiting. Instead, Fabiola preferred to choose an expert, rather than a courtier, to accompany her on her various duties.

A caring Queen

But for some of her activities she needed no adviser. Her hospital training stood her in good stead for the increasing amount of time she spent with handicapped children. She needed no help for the long hours during which she poured over art history books or played classical music on her guitar. As Baudouin liked to say of his wife, 'What is marvellous about the Queen is that she is totally authentic.'

Not all members of the family were as responsible as Baudouin and Fabiola. In 1964, Baudouin's young half-brother Prince Alexandre failed his medical exams and was packed off to Harvard. Brussels, however, seemed to have a magnetic hold on Alexandre. Four times that December he flew back home without telling his family. On one trip he dyed his hair to avoid recognition. The police, however, saw through his disguise and alerted his family. The next morning, Princess Liliane personally escorted

him – freshly shampooed – back to the airport.

But when he was spotted, the following January, gambling in a Brussels nightclub and disappearing in his Ferrari in the early hours of the morning with a leggy blonde, Baudouin himself had to intervene. The King was reported to be deeply embarrassed by Alexandre's activities, and the 22-year-old Prince was packed, unshaven, on to the next plane for America.

Black sheep of the family
Then, as if his own family was not bad enough, Baudouin also had to deal with Fabiola's. By now, her brother Jaime had parted company with one wife, three jazz bands, several nightclubs and a large part of his personal fortune. 'After a single year in America,' Jaime proudly told the press, 'I managed to get through my entire inheritance of 36 million pesetas. When that had gone I didn't even have the money for my return ticket, so for eight months I worked in the port of New York, opening packing cases for seven dollars a day.' Newspapers took great delight in picturing him, with his new Swedish wife, peering hungrily through the railings of the Royal Palace – whose inhabitants adamantly refused to let him in.

Nor did Baudouin approve of Jaime's musical career, which had spawned such numbers as 'Fabiola', 'Waltz of the Queen' and, the King suspected, though Jaime denied it, the 'Baudouin Cha-Cha-Cha'. By 1963 Jaime had found gainful employment with a Swiss-based company as Director of International Affairs. As he hoisted his alligator loafers on to the table at an interview, he claimed, 'I have finished with the high life. I have been a great embarrassment to my family. Now I

⚜**Above** *Former British Prime Minister Harold Macmillan greets the Belgian Royal couple at a reception in 1972. Whatever the event, Fabiola is usually to be found at Baudouin's side*

must pull myself together.' But upright Belgians would have shuddered to know that the new product he had just demonstrated at a press conference – a pop bottle with a built-in straw – was actually filled with whisky.

Such worries, however, were soon swept to

INTO THE 'SEVENTIES

Baudouin and Fabiola emerged from the Swinging 'Sixties into a decade of inflation, unemployment and universal disillusionment. But the experience of the last years had prepared them well, though Fabiola's sad Spanish eyes seemed sadder still. Baudouin, always grave, now took on the image of a perfect, upright and unemotional monarch. To other Europeans, who followed the activities of their remaining royal families with prurient zest, he was downright boring. Britain's *Financial Times* described him as having 'all the charisma of a bank manager'.

A country split in two

But if Baudouin was a bank manager, he was taking good care of his people's personal accounts. He and Fabiola now dedicated themselves to their country, taking a particular interest in religion and children. Their enthusiasm was a boon for their countrymen.

Belgium had long been a nation composed of uneasy alliances. The national borders enclosed a shaky mish-mash of racial divisions. There were 'guest workers' from Africa and elsewhere; there was a sizeable German population;

one side. For on 9 July 1966, it was announced that Fabiola was once again with child. Tragically, only two days later Fabiola was rushed to hospital to have an ectopic pregnancy terminated. The operation effectively ended Fabiola's last chance of having a child.

👑**Above** *The King and Queen wave to a cheering crowd from a balcony of the Brussels Town Hall. It is 1976 and Baudouin is celebrating 25 years on the throne of Belgium. Thanks to Baudouin's steadiness of character, he had enjoyed a much smoother reign than anyone could have forecast in 1951. Marrying Fabiola left was a smart move. She quickly became very popular and commands great respect from the Belgian people. Princess Paola right, married to Baudouin's brother Albert, was not so fortunate. She was castigated by press and public over the state of her marriage and her inability to learn Flemish. But now she and Albert are happily married and she is almost as fervent a Catholic as Fabiola*

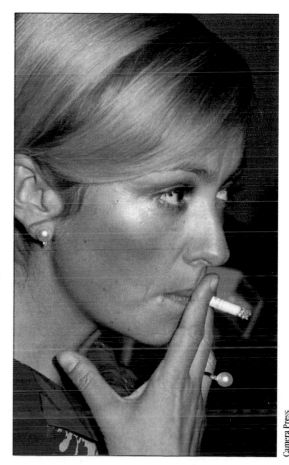

> '*What is marvellous about the Queen is that she is totally authentic*'
>
> BAUDOUIN ON FABIOLA

Belga

but most notably there were the Dutch-speaking Flemings and the French-speaking Walloons. An undercurrent of nationalistic rivalry under-pinned life, and arguments as to which language should be used and where, from street signs to legal documents, were widespread.

Accordingly, the monarchy was the linch-pin that held the country together. Being neither Walloon or Fleming – the Coburgs were of German origin – Baudouin was seen as having a degree of impartiality. The Belgian people were glad to see that he was giving his undiv-ided, and dutiful, attention to the country.

Baudouin to the rescue

The people were glad, too, that Fabiola took the same line. Shortly after the Royal marriage, Belgium had been swept by a wave of disasters: the southern part of the country had been stricken by floods, a village in the east had been buried by a slag heap, and a Belgian airliner had crashed with the loss of 73 lives. Fabiola had appeared at the scene of each disaster alongside her husband. It was an attention to duty that she never relinquished. Moreover, her position in the hearts and minds of the predominantly Catholic Belgians was reinforced by her strong faith. She took Baudouin to Mass every day, had a private oratory built in the grounds of the palace at Laeken, and would frequently invite the Belgian primate to dinner.

Princess Paola in trouble

This was in sharp contrast to what the Belgians could glean of the activities of the rest of the Royal Family. The glamorous Princess Paola (mar-ried to Prince Albert), while stunning Belgian society with her good looks and fashionable hairstyles, fell short of the high standards set by the Queen. One of Fabiola's first duties had been to add Flemish to her list of languages. Italian-born Paola, however, found this difficult. In 1967, she had attended just four hour-long lessons

Popperfoto

*♛Above **Baudouin stands between his sister Josephine-Charlotte, Grand Duchess of Luxemburg, and a heavily veiled Princess Liliane at the funeral of his father. The much-maligned Leopold III died in September 1983, aged 81. After a funeral service in Brussels, Leopold was laid to rest in the family crypt at Laeken. The funeral brought together the whole family as they mourned the ex-King: Fabiola even took the arm of Liliane, from whom she had been estranged for a long time. Leopold's brother Charles had died earlier the same year***

before giving it up. The following year, however, as criticism began to swell among the Flemings, politicians advised her to make another attempt. Accordingly, she was bundled off to a Dutch con-vent for a three-day crash course.

But what worried Belgians more than her inability to speak the language, was the disas-trous state of her marriage. In 1970, under the assumed name of Madame Legrand, she flew to Sardinia where she was pictured strolling hand in hand with a bearded stranger. The floodgates of gossip burst open. It was remembered that she had never liked the formality of royal duties. It was recalled that a Vatican policeman had turned her away from St Peter's because her miniskirt was too short. Rumours began to surface about her friendship with a pop singer. Papers pointed out that she and Albert lived in different wings of the Royal Palace and that they had not had a holiday together for two years.

When the press had exhausted the subject of Paola, they turned on Albert. For some years now, Albert had been almost continuously abroad, making promotional tours for Belgian industry. Belgian officials, it was said, had reacted with stern disapproval to pictures of him at nightclubs in Tokyo and elsewhere. It was also claimed that he had a long-standing relationship with a 20-year-old salesgirl from a Brussels store.

The Belgian authorities were quick to act. The police searched newspaper offices for copies of the picture of Paola, and issued warnings of stern reprisals should the banned

photographs be published. Baudouin took it upon himself to warn Albert and Paola that their primary duty lay to Belgium, not to their private lives. And on Paola's 32nd birthday, he summoned the couple to his holiday home in Malaga, in the hope that he could turn the celebrations into a family reconciliation. But the following day it was reported that the two had gone their separate ways.

Uncle Charles

Then the rumours began about Baudouin's uncle, Prince Charles. In October 1970, the unconfirmed news emerged that the 67 year-old Prince had married his secretary Karin Vernooy, the 27-year-old daughter of a bulb farmer. A little later it was announced that Charles was the father of an illegitimate daughter.

Fortunately for Baudouin there was less need to step in. Prince Charles soon retired from the public eye, becoming an almost total recluse

👑 Top right *Baudouin and Fabiola with King Juan Carlos and Queen Sofia of Spain, relaxing together at Laeken. Baudouin and Juan Carlos have much in common: both are Catholic monarchs whose early years were spent in uncertainty and even danger*

👑 *Baudouin and Fabiola* above *walking together at Ciergnon in the Ardennes. The couple divide their time between the Royal Palace in Brussels, Laeken, Ciergnon and Opgrimbie in northern Belgium*

👑 *Princess Marie Christine* right, *the elder daughter of Leopold and Liliane, hit the headlines in 1981 when she married a Toronto bar-pianist, Paul Drake. Her family were appalled but 'We are very much in love and fabulously happy,' the Princess claimed. But just six weeks later the marriage was over*

PAGE 24 — Daily Mail, Thursday, April 5, 1990

CHILDREN A KING AND QUEEN SO LONGED FOR BUT NEVER HAD SPARK AN 'ABDICATION'

The heartbreak behind a royal crisis of conscience

By RICHARD KAY
Royal Correspondent

Baudouin stands down over law allowing abortion

sentence. Baudouin is also protected by another piece of archaic legislation called *Offence au Roi*. The law, which makes it an offence to commit 'outrage' against the monarchy, has never been repealed.

In the early weeks of 1990, it was dusted down and put into action. When giving his Christmas speech of 1989, Baudouin had made his main topic the sanctity of family life and children's rights. To a lawyer from Namur, Christian Bouvier, this was too much. Why, he asked, had Baudouin not mentioned the revolutions that were bringing Eastern European countries clanging through the Iron Curtain? The King, he warned, should 'prepare for the Republic'.

Monsieur Bouvier received just one reply to his letter. It came from the public prosecutor, who informed him that he was charged with 'outrage', and would face prosecution and compulsory psychiatric examination for mental

♔**Above** *On Tuesday 3 April 1990 the news flashed round the world that Baudouin had abdicated. But just two days later he was reinstated. He had temporarily stepped down to avoid approving a bill legalizing abortion, which became law in his absence. The bill had been passed by the Belgian Senate, but Baudouin's conscience would not allow him to sign it, and so this ingenious way of getting around the constitutional impasse was devised. Five months later the Belgian King celebrated his 60th birthday and 39 years on the throne* right

who devoted his time to collecting books on the sea and amassing a household of valuable *objets d'art*. Only on rare occasions did he hit the headlines, such as when he was the victim of a serious fraud, when he was discovered wandering around the streets of Brussels in a rather dazed fashion, and when it was revealed that he was a practising homosexual.

Family resemblance

1983 saw the deaths of both Charles and Leopold. The old generation was passing away. But in the minds of some it still lingered on in the King himself. Many were interested to see that Baudouin was becoming increasingly like his grandfather, King Albert – especially since he had exchanged his spectacles for more youthful-looking contact lenses. He has the same profile, the same manner of walking with his hands behind his back, and the same interest in science and technology.

Beyond such comparisons, however, Belgians know strangely little about their King and Queen. In part this is because Baudouin and Fabiola prefer to remain private people. Largely, however, it is because of an ancient law that bans all reports other than those of official engagements, under threat of a three-year prison